Tales From Working on a Dude Ranch

A Journey of Adventure and Gratitude

By Richard V Dalke, MS

Tales From Working on a Dude Ranch

Richard V. Dalke

Umatilla River at the Bar M Ranch

A Short History

The Bar M Ranch has a rich and interesting history. The three story hand hewn building known as the Ranch House was built in 1864 as a stage coach stop for the California Stage Company. This stop was along the historic Thomas-Ruckel Road which served as a mail route from Boise, Idaho to Walla Walla, Washington.

Tales From Working on a Dude Ranch

Richard V. Dalke

Prior to the Baker's buying the ranch, it was known as Bingham Springs and was owned by Dr. Bingham from 1892 to 1908. The hot springs flowed out of the mountain side and into the pool, where visitors would come for the day to enjoy what was believed to be healing mineral waters. Some famous guests include Presidents Calvin Coolidge and Herbert Hoover.

Dr. Bingham added a 2 story building a short distance from the Ranch House that was known as the "Annex." Later the second story was taken down, but the rest of the building remained as additional housing for the guests. A few cabins were also built, one called Lakeside, which was next to the little man-made lake built by the Bakers, sometimes with a little help from the local beavers. The Brookside cabin was built a little closer to the

Tales From Working on a Dude Ranch

Richard V. Dalke

Ranch House, alongside the small brook that carried the water from the lake down past the Ranch House and other buildings, eventually returning to the river after being used to irrigate the lawns on the ranch.

Several other owners purchased and sold the property after Dr. Bingham until Howard and Bonnie Baker bought it in 1938 and named it the Bar M Ranch. They started operating it as a dude ranch in the 1940's. Howard had surprised Bonnie with the purchase of the ranch after traveling far and wide trying to find the perfect place to settle down and raise a family.

They had two children – Gene and Virginia (known as 'Gina'). Gene stayed on the ranch after he married Hope, doing much of the maintenance, horseshoeing and eventually the cooking for the guests. To avoid confusion of who was to be called

Tales From Working on a Dude Ranch

Richard V. Dalke

Mr. and Mrs. Baker, Howard and Bonnie became known simply as Mr. and Mrs. 'B'.

Gene and Hope Baker helped run the ranch along with their four children - Dan, Sally, Jerry and Tom.

The stories in this book took place during this period of time when the Bakers ran the ranch, from the early 1970's to the mid 1990's.

Tales From Working on a Dude Ranch

Richard V. Dalke

ISBN-10: 1495249727

ISBN-13: 978-1495249723

Published by Deerhawk Enterprises, LLC 2014

PO Box 9113, Spokane, WA 99209

Richard V. Dalke

Dedication

To the Baker family who ran the Bar M Guest Ranch for over half a century and who made it possible for me to experience all of the interesting adventures that I write about in this book.

Tales From Working on a Dude Ranch

Richard V. Dalke

Richard V. Dalke

Other books by Richard Dalke

A Diary in Haiku

7 months in Poetry

Also available as an audiobook.

Angels & Air Machines

A book for children

Indelible Ink

Expanding Awareness Through Poetry

Musings & Metaphors

A book of Daily Wisdom

Journey Through a Writing Class

Short Stories for Teens

Tales From Working on a Dude Ranch

Richard V. Dalke

Each of these books are available through amazon.com,
other book retailers or from my website at
deerhawkenterprises.com.

Richard V. Dalke

Preface

I first started working on the Bar M Dude (Guest) Ranch as a wrangler when I was 19 years old. I worked there for three years – usually from March through the first part of September. After these three seasons, I returned for a few days to a week at a time many times to either help out or as a paying guest.

I was not able to locate all of the folks mentioned in my stories to get permission to use their name, so some of the names in the book have been changed or only their first names were used.

Tales From Working on a Dude Ranch

Richard V. Dalke

Each of the experiences written about in this book actually happened, though the chapters are not necessarily in chronological order. My memory of incidents that took place over 40 years ago may differ slightly from the memories of the other participants. My apologies if that has happened.

Acknowledgements

I would like to thank my wife – Kayte Ross - for supporting me in the writing of this as well as my other books and recordings.

TABLE OF CONTENTS

Tales From Working on a Dude Ranch

Richard V. Dalke

Tales From Working on a Dude Ranch

Richard V. Dalke

Tales From Working on a Dude Ranch

Richard V. Dalke

Richard V. Dalke

Chapter 1

A Desire is Born

The desire to work on a ranch started when I was 15 years old. I lived in Spokane, Washington, a mid-sized city in the Pacific Northwest and wanted to get a summer job working with horses. My brothers and I had helped out on our Granddad's dairy farm on weekends, cutting wood, driving tractors and feeding the calves. They had one Shetland pony on the farm, which we rode a few times, but I wanted to learn more about training and riding full sized horses. I also wanted to earn enough money to buy a nice car.

I'd gone horse-back riding a number of times at several stables on the outskirts of town. I liked the horses and the trails at one of those stables, so I chose that one as a possible place to work for the summer. It was about 5 miles from where I lived on the South Hill and not on any of the bus routes.

I wanted to look the part, but the only things I owned that looked the least bit western were an old pair of cowboy boots, a straw hat, denim jeans and a large rodeo style belt buckle. The heels of the boots were so worn the nails jutted into the bottom of my feet whenever I wore them. Even so, my desire to look like a cowboy was stronger than my concern about my feet, so I put the jeans, hat, boots and fancy belt buckle on and headed out the door.

Tales From Working on a Dude Ranch

Richard V. Dalke

Not having any transportation, I decided to walk the 5 miles. Every step of the way I could feel the tips of the nails jabbing into my heels.

After about two hours of walking, I arrived at the riding stables and walked up to the lady who looked like she ran the place.

"Hi, my name is Dick and I'd like to work here. You might recognize me, since I've come here a lot to ride your horses."

"Do you have any experience working with horses or in taking out trail rides?" she asked.

"I used to work on my Granddad's dairy farm and I've ridden a few dozen times at yours and some other stables down the road, but I haven't ever taken out trail rides or trained horses or anything. I'm willing to learn and I'm a hard worker." I offered hopefully.

"I'm sorry," she replied, "we only hire wranglers that have worked a lot with horses. Too

Richard V. Dalke

many potential dangers. We don't want anyone getting hurt. Good luck, though."

"Ok, thanks," I muttered, feeling dejected.

I turned to head back home. On the spot, I made a promise to myself that somehow, someday, I would become so good at working with horses, that they would wish they could hire me. In my mind I was of course thinking that if that ever happened, I would have to turn them down.

With pain in my heart, and pain in my heels, I walked the five miles back home, disappointed but determined.

A few weeks later, I was asked to work full time for my Granddad on his dairy farm, hauling hay and milking cows. At the end of the summer, I was invited to move in with them and work during the school year while going to Cheney High School - a new High School for me. I earned enough money to buy my first car – a 1957 Chevy Bel Air.

Richard V. Dalke

Little did I know at the time, that within 4 years, my dream of working on a ranch with cattle and lots of horses would come true.

Chapter 2

A Long Term Relationship Begins

I sat on my undersized bed, not much bigger than a cot, and stared out of the window of the bunk house. I could hear the mares whinnying for their hay. I'd get to them in a minute, but first I wanted to think something through. I'd worked hard driving truck and taking care of the horses for the college all summer, living in a little one room shed that was part of the University's stable. I'd taken my horsemanship classes there, joined the rodeo club and met some interesting girls.

I glanced at the calendar on the wall. Two weeks before school starts. Time to do something fun. Sharon, one of the girls I'd met in the rodeo club had told me to come up and see her sometime. She lived about sixty miles north of my hometown, and about 150 miles from the college. But I was afraid I'd get all tongue-tied when I saw her again, just like the first time I'd met her. Recalling the day, I could feel my face flush. I was determined to get over my shyness before I finished college. I made a decision. Tomorrow morning my two week vacation would start. I was going to head north to the little town of Addy, Washington. I couldn't wait to see the surprise on Sharon's face.

I finished my chores, ate some dinner and went to bed early. By 7:00 the next morning I was in my car, a 1962 Chevy Nova that I'd bought with

Richard V. Dalke

the $900 I'd earned hauling hay the summer before plus my '57 Chevy as a trade in. By 8:30 I'd driven through my hometown, and headed north toward Addy. I was feeling adventurous.

About an hour later, I pulled into a dilapidated Texaco gas station on the edge of the small town where Sharon lived.

"Why sure," the elderly man attending the station answered, wiping the grease off his hands with a grungy looking bandanna he pulled from his back pocket. "The Saunders' place is just over the hill, turn right and then 'bout a quarter of a mile past the water tower. It's an old white house with dairy barns and a long dusty driveway leading up to it. You can't miss it." To show my appreciation, I filled up my gas tank from his pump and headed for the Saunders' farm.

I drove past the water tower, saw the white house and stopped at the mail box alongside the road and read the names, Vi and Harold Saunders, the red letters beginning to peel. I began wondering what I was doing. Was I crazy? I couldn't just drive up to somebody's place that I didn't know and ask them where their daughter was. I pulled my car to a shady spot under an old elm tree about a quarter mile down the road and continued waging the verbal battle in my mind. Finally, after about fifteen minutes, I lumbered back to the Saunders' driveway and drove slowly up to the house. My hands were sweating.

An older man with a slight limp came out of the house. "Get down, Jasper and Honey," he hollered at the dogs. "What can I do for you son?" he said.

"Hi, my name's Dick and I went to college this past year with your daughter, Sharon. She said if I was ever up in her area to drop in and say hello. You must be her dad."

Tales From Working on a Dude Ranch

Richard V. Dalke

"Yep, I'm her dad and you've got the right place, but Sharon's gone for the summer." He spat a chew of tobacco close to my left foot. "She didn't tell me about no boy she met at school, so you best be getting along."

"You're probably right," I answered, then added, "that's a mighty nice Australian Shepherd you got there," pointing to the gray and white dog with one pale eye and one blue one. "We used to have one just like her on the dairy farm I lived on. They sure make good cow dogs."

"You know something about cow dogs and dairy farmin' huh," the older man replied. "I thought maybe you was just a city kid. You can call me Hank." He shook my hand. She's working for a dude ranch in the Blue Mountains of Oregon, not too far from Pendleton. I don't recall what the name of the place is, just exactly."

Tales From Working on a Dude Ranch

Richard V. Dalke

"Thanks a lot Hank," I answered. "I can find it." I walked back to my car, sat in the front seat and looked at the map. Pendleton was about five hours from Addy, approximately 120 miles south of the college I'd left that morning. I drove back to the highway, stopped once more at the Texaco station, this time to pick up a cold can of Squirt, and headed south toward Oregon.

I went back through my hometown, onto Highway 95, drove south about fifty miles to Colfax and turned west. I kept wondering what I would say to Sharon when I saw her again. I practiced several scripts over in my mind, each one more friendly and nonchalant than the last. I drove through several small towns, and several hours later, through Walla Walla and then into Pendleton. I stopped at a small café for a BLT on whole wheat, gulped it down with another Squirt and looked for a phone booth. I found one close to a Safeway store. I scanned the

Richard V. Dalke

yellow pages and found two dude ranches listed. I tried the first one – the Bar M.

Hope Baker answered the phone. "Yes, we do have a girl named Sharon that works here, but she's not at the ranch today. She's in Pendleton, shopping for groceries at the Safeway store. Sorry. She's with Susie, another girl that works here and they'll be driving a blue Volvo with a Bar M brand painted on the side. They might still be there, if you hurry."

I felt deflated. I started back toward my car when I noticed a blue Volvo station wagon in the parking lot with lettering painted on the door. I went closer. It was the Bar M brand! My heart started pounding. Sharon was probably right here. I took a deep breath and walked inside. I saw her with another girl that looked about the same age walking down the produce aisle. They stopped at the watermelons. My shyness suddenly came back full

Tales From Working on a Dude Ranch

Richard V. Dalke

force. My hands were sweating. My mouth felt like dry cotton. I'd just driven over four hundred miles and now I couldn't bring my legs to move twenty feet closer to her. I could feel the heat rise to my face both from embarrassment and anger at myself. I retreated to a greeting card display that was close to where they were standing and positioned myself behind it, pretending to look intently for a birthday card for one of my sisters. It was close to her birthday, I remembered, though I'd rarely bought her a birthday card before. I could hear Sharon whispering to her friend.

"Hey, I know that guy over there. He was in some of my classes at college last year."

I watched them put a few more groceries in their cart and head for the checkout stand. I knew in my heart that I was perfectly willing to walk right out of the store and drive four hours all the way back to the bunkhouse and my undersized bed at the

Tales From Working on a Dude Ranch

Richard V. Dalke

University. If this was something that was meant to be, I rationalized to myself, it should happen naturally. I could see them start to take their groceries out of the cart. Slowly, like a cowboy who's climbing back on the horse that just threw him, I picked out a card and shuffled toward the same cashier that Sharon and her friend were at. I caught Sharon's eye.

"Hi Dick," she said, smiling. "What are you doing here?"

"Oh, I was just in town and I remembered it was close to my sister's birthday, so I picked out a card for her." I showed them the card I'd picked out, trying hard not to blush.

"Susie and I work at a really neat dude ranch only thirty miles or so from town. You ought to come out and see it." Sharon nodded toward her friend and smiled again.

Tales From Working on a Dude Ranch

Richard V. Dalke

"Ok, that'd be great. I've always wanted to see a dude ranch. Maybe I could follow you out there," I replied, starting to feel a little more comfortable.

I drove behind the blue Volvo for thirty-three miles, traveling deeper and deeper into the Blue Mountains. Along the way I saw a farm with buffalo on it, and high on the hillside, several deer and a herd of elk. When we got to the Bar M, Sharon introduced me to the Bakers, took me on a short ride, and told me about the ranch's history.

"How long do most of the dudes stay?" I asked, still feeling self-conscious.

"We call them guests, not dudes, since many of them are experienced riders. They usually stay for a week, sometimes two." Sharon responded, a little impatiently. She continued to tell me about the ranch. "That stream we crossed was really the Umatilla River which flows right through the

Tales From Working on a Dude Ranch

Richard V. Dalke

Baker's property and they have a natural warm-springs swimming pool and miles of beautiful riding trails."

She sounded a bit like a recorded tour guide, I thought, but didn't say anything. We rode for another half hour while Sharon continued to talk about the ranch and I continued to listen. We crossed the river one more time and headed back. After unsaddling our horses and leading them into the corral, Sharon looked at me and answered the question that had been on my mind.

"I talked to Hope when we brought the groceries in. She said it would be Ok for you to spend the night, if you don't mind sleeping in the storage room. There's an extra cot in there. It's just down the hall from Susie's and my apartment in that red building next to the cabins. We call it the Annex." She pointed toward a long maroon colored

Richard V. Dalke

building partially hidden behind a row of blackberry bushes and several tall Locust trees.

I stayed that night and the rest of the week as a guest, spending most of my summer's savings. Then I remained another seven days as an unpaid wrangler, working with the young colts and building trails. Each time I tried talking to Sharon, I realized how different we were. I knew that we would never be more than friends, but I was falling in love with the Bar M. Two weeks later, when it was time to leave, I gave my favorite horse a hug and shook Sharon's hand goodbye. I knew I'd be back many times to see the ranch and the Bakers.

Richard V. Dalke

Chapter 3

Dynamite Story

The next Spring, I talked to Mr. Baker, who everyone called "Mr. B" about working on the ranch for the summer, letting him know I was willing to work for just room and board. I was 20 years old, and willing to experience something fun, even if I didn't earn any money for it.

I also wanted to see Sharon again, to see if there was the possibility of rekindling any sparks.

Tales From Working on a Dude Ranch

Richard V. Dalke

I started in March, a couple of months before the guests and kitchen help arrived, preparing the trails, clearing brush, working with the young colts and fillies and riding the 2 and 3 year olds, preparing them for the riders coming in June.

I'd been there several weeks, working with Mr. B on the trails. My job was to scrape out the small rocks and debris that poured out of the holes he was drilling into the mountainside with the gas-powered pneumatic drill he operated. We'd place a stick or two of dynamite in each hole, connect each stick with a line of the explosive Prima-cord and attach the cord to a blasting cap. We used the type of dynamite that blasted down into the mountain, loosening the rocks and breaking up the boulders. Then we'd clear out the debris, placing the medium sized rocks along the edge. The rocks helped keep the horses on the inside of the path, so the riders

Richard V. Dalke

would feel safe as well as making the trails last longer for the hundreds of rides we'd go on each season.

Mr. B showed me how to place the dynamite in the holes, stick the Prima-cord into the end of each one and roll it out a safe distance from the blast to come. Our horses were always tied up some distance off, reducing the chances of them bolting and the two of us having to walk back down the mountain. To protect ourselves, we hid behind a large Ponderosa Pine tree before touching off the dynamite.

After watching Mr. B prepare the dynamite several times, he let me do it. We'd always shout ***"BLASTING"*** when it was time to set off the explosion. I enjoyed working with the dynamite, always taking the necessary precautions.

After two months of working with the dynamite and getting the trails ready, I looked

Richard V. Dalke

forward to Sharon coming back to the ranch and excited to impress her with what I'd learned.

It was early June, a few days before the first guests of the season were scheduled to arrive. Sharon returned to the ranch, to help in the kitchen and prepare the cabins for the guests. The kitchen help didn't have to work in the afternoons after lunch, so she could be available for a ride. One of those afternoons, I asked Sharon if she was interested in riding with me up Rock Creek on the north side of the river for some trail clearing work. She was about to say yes, when I mentioned that I would be using dynamite to blast out a large stump that was blocking part of the trail.

"I don't think so," she said. "Seems a little too dangerous to me."

"I always pack the blasting caps and Prima-cord on one side of the saddle and the dynamite on the other. They can't touch each other. We should

Richard V. Dalke

be safe enough." I smiled, more nervous about asking her to go with me than about the safety of the dynamite.

"Thanks anyway," she said, "not today."

I finished packing the blasting caps, the battery, the Prima-cord and the dynamite into the saddle bags and headed up the trail alone. After about a half hour of riding, I found the tree trunk that was blocking the path. I tied my gelding to a tree a little over 50 yards away and around a curve at a safe distance from the blast to come.

I dug under the tree stump, packed in two or three sticks of the dynamite and connected the Prima-cord and blasting cap to each other. We had usually used the type of dynamite that blasted down into the hole, loosening rock and hard dirt to widen the trail. This time I used the kind that blasted up and out, as I wanted to blast the stump out of the earth, hopefully knocking it out of way of the trail.

Tales From Working on a Dude Ranch

Richard V. Dalke

I went around the bend, close to where my pony stood, in case I needed to calm him down and stood behind a large tree. I pulled the battery out of my pocket, and prepared to set off the dynamite. I hollered out "***BLASTING,***" as I was trained to do, even though I was pretty sure there weren't any other riders on the mountain.

When I touched the wires of the blasting cap to the head of the battery, I heard a thunderous **BANG** and then several seconds later a loud **THUMP**. The stump not only blew out of the mountainside, it flew through the air, clear across Rock Creek, landing just below the trail on the other side of the canyon.

Good thing I'd remembered how to tie a knot that my dad had taught me years earlier. I'd used a clove hitch to tie my pony to a tree – a knot that held strong enough to keep him from escaping and from me needing to walk down the mountain

Richard V. Dalke

back to the ranch house. Too bad Sharon hadn't come on the ride with me – I felt pretty sure she would've been impressed with my new found skills.

When I told her the story later, she stared up at me, her eyes open wide, not with eyes of wonderment, but with a 'are you crazy' kind of look on her face.

I knew right then it was time for me to look elsewhere for a girlfriend.

Richard V. Dalke

Chapter 4

The Dining Room

Gene – Mr. and Mrs. B's son – was the primary cook, with lots of help from his wife, Hope, Bonny, his mother, and the hired kitchen help. I'd heard that they had hired a cook several times in the past, but had problems finding one that would be reliable enough to drive over 30 miles each day to and from the ranch in time to get the cooking done. So years earlier, they made the decision to have Gene trade in his horseshoeing apron for a cooking apron. He knew how to cook

Richard V. Dalke

finger-licking-good fried chicken, special Bar M salad, homemade dinner rolls, cinnamon rolls, mashed potatoes, baked spaghetti, roast pork and many other delightful treats. Every meal was delicious. It was a good thing we had hard physical work to do on a daily basis, keeping us fit enough to swing into the saddle each morning.

Gene also raised his own raspberry bushes in his huge garden and was well known throughout the county for making some of the best raspberry jam within 100 miles. Guests and neighbors alike would come to the ranch and order jars of the delicious frozen spread to take home with them.

Many of the guests listed the homemade cooking as one of the main reasons for coming to the ranch each year and certainly became one of the main reasons that I returned for those many years.

Dan – Gene and Hope's oldest son – and I often would challenge each other during the meals

Tales From Working on a Dude Ranch

Richard V. Dalke

we ate at the ranch. We often sat across from each other in the dining hall. Whenever one of us asked the other to pass the pitcher of ice water or lemonade or juice, we were more than happy to oblige. But instead of passing the pitcher, we would fill the other's glass as full as we could possibly get it. The challenge for the pourer was to fill the glass as close to the top as possible without spilling over. If it dribbled over the edge, you 'lost.'

The challenge for the recipient was to pick up the drink and get it all the way to his mouth and drink it without spilling a drop. Of course the more nonchalant and stable you were at achieving either task, the better.

By the end of the summer, both of us had become experts at the game, each with a steady hand, neither of us losing a drop of liquid either from pouring or from drinking.

Tales From Working on a Dude Ranch

Richard V. Dalke

From time to time something embarrassing would happen in the dining room. Not only the dropping of a plate or the crash of silverware, which was to be expected in any kitchen, but sometimes incidents we found humorous.

Hope was a stickler for correct manners at the table, reminding us to eat with our mouth closed, to keep our elbows off the table and to always speak appropriately to the guests.

It was a Sunday afternoon, the first meal of the week, after the new guests for the week had just checked into their rooms. One of Hope's jobs was assigning the accommodations for each family and checking later to make sure they found their correct rooms.

A husband and wife in their 50's were sitting next to me and a young couple with a 9 year old boy sat across the table. All were enjoying their meal. Hope came out of the kitchen and approached

Richard V. Dalke

the table, carrying a tray of fresh dinner rolls and looked at the older couple.

"You two are in room number 8, is that right?" she asked.

"No," the wife answered. "We're in 7." The young couple looked up at Hope and exclaimed in unison. – "we are."

"Oh, so you're in 8," Hope replied. As soon as she said it, she realized how that phrase sounded like something you do in the bathroom – and turned beet red. She placed the tray on the table and hurried back to the kitchen, too embarrassed to come back out until lunch was over.

I don't think either couple realized why Hope left the table in such a hurry. Each of them grabbed a fresh roll, spread on a pat of butter with raspberry jam and continued eating their meal. I looked over at Dan and saw a knowing smile on his face. We never mentioned it to Hope. We didn't want to embarrass her again.

Richard V. Dalke

Chapter 5

Earning an Income

My agreement with Mr. B was to work for just room and board, since I knew I didn't have a lot of experience training horses or building trail. One morning after I'd been working there for about 6 weeks, I was asked to go to the corral to pick out a couple of horses for riding and a third one to use as a pack horse to carry the jack hammer. I walked the quarter mile down to the hay barn, and looked the horses over. I picked out an appaloosa named Eagle, a gentle gelding we

Richard V. Dalke

could use for a pack horse. I came up to him with a small 'horse goody' – a small Lincoln log sized treat made from oats and molasses – in my hand to get him to come to me.

I placed one end of the lead rope around his neck, tied a bowline knot and threaded the other end of the rope through the loop so that the rope wouldn't slip too tight around his neck. I tied him to a pole and went to choose two other horses. The two mares I was looking for were close by and they came right up to me seeking the treats. I tied a rope around each of their necks as well and led them back to where Eagle was tied. I wrapped the lead rope over the gelding's nose and jumped on him bareback, leading the other two horses behind me. I opened the gate and led the mares through, closing the gate behind me without letting any of the other horses out. It had taken several weeks for me to accomplish that feat without mishap.

Tales From Working on a Dude Ranch

Richard V. Dalke

I started back down the road and headed for the feed bunks next to the tack room.

About half way there, a neighbor's dog ran out and started barking wildly, frightening the two horses I was leading and making them pull back violently.

I was yanked off Eagle, landed on a rock and injured my shoulder. Gene came running out of the house and helped me up and brushed me off. He could tell I was in pain, so he drove me to the local hospital in Pendleton, where they x-rayed me and told me I had dislocated my shoulder. Gene filled out the paperwork for Worker's Compensation which would pay for the hospital bill. I didn't know it at the time, but filling out that paperwork indicated that I was an employee, eligible to earn a paycheck. Gene hadn't known about my deal with Mr. B – working for only board and room – so I

Richard V. Dalke

was now eligible to earn an income – getting paid the same as the other wranglers on the ranch.

I didn't make a lot – $100 a month to start, but I was grateful to become a paid wrangler – getting a monthly paycheck, a small cabin to sleep in, wonderful meals and eligible for tips from the guests. Gene was kind enough to explain the situation to Mr. B who reluctantly agreed to the new arrangement.

Chapter 6

"I Think She's Going Over"

Getting a curve on a hill named after you is always an honor. A curve on the Thornhollow grade was named after me during a summer season in the early 1970's.

We'd started out early that morning after breakfast. We'd eaten baked eggs with bacon, sourdough biscuits and pancakes. Dan, Jerry and I went down to the rec barn where we parked the 2½ ton truck we used for hauling hay, cattle, gravel and

Richard V. Dalke

other miscellaneous loads that were needed on the ranch.

This particular morning, we took off the racks and got the truck ready for hauling a load of hay bales. Before the day was over we would learn another lesson: it's important to stabilize a truck bed that has a hydraulic lift on it.

We were picking up the hay from a farmer some 30 miles or so north of the Bar M. I got in the driver's side of the truck, as I was the only one with a driver's license. I started up the engine and we headed down the road toward Athena. This meant driving up the Thornhollow grade, a hill with a number of switchbacks and hairpin curves, overlooking a canyon several hundred feet below. No problem going up the hill – the truck was empty. Coming back down would be a different story.

We went to the hay farm and stacked 5 tiers of alfalfa-grass bales onto the truck - a full load. I'd

Tales From Working on a Dude Ranch

Richard V. Dalke

spent years stacking and hauling hay on my Grandfather's dairy farm, so knew how to stack the bales in a pattern that interlocked them in and kept the load balanced.

We tied the load down with heavy duty ropes tied to the front of the truck bed. We pulled them over the top of the hay bales and tied them in the back using a loop in the rope that helped us pull them snug.

We got back in the truck and headed for home. I drove at the speed limit along the main roads and slowed way down when we approached the Thornhollow grade. Most of the hill had a 30 mile an hour speed limit, some of the switchbacks had signs indicating 20 or slower.

We were about half way down the hill when we started around one of the hairpin switchbacks. We were going no more than 20 miles per hour when the truck started to creak and tip over. I

Richard V. Dalke

stepped on the brakes, but we continued tipping over to my side of the truck – into the hillside. We looked over the cliff on our right, hundreds of feet down the canyon. We thanked our lucky stars that the truck tipped into the mountain instead of the other direction.

"Hold on boys, I think we're going over." I shouted. Sure enough the entire load and the truck tipped over. The bed of the truck had come loose. Bales of hay were all over the road.

Dan knew the neighbor at the bottom of the hill, so he walked down to let someone at the ranch know what had happened. While waiting for someone to come, we took the rest of the hay off the truck, so we'd be able to tip the truck back upright. The tipping had happened so slowly that no damage was done to the truck.

Once we took the hay off, the truck sprang back to level. We were lucky it didn't flip all the

Tales From Working on a Dude Ranch

Richard V. Dalke

way over into the canyon on the other side of the road. We reloaded all of the hay and tied it down again. We climbed into the cab and drove very slowly the rest of the way back to the ranch. The bell rang just as we passed under the Bar M sign at the head of the quarter-mile long driveway, indicating it was time for lunch. After parking the truck and washing up, we went in to join the others for the noon meal.

In between bites of homemade tacos and sips of lemonade, we told the wide-eyed guests and staff what had happened.

"Another story to tell the grandkids," Gene quipped, poking his head out from the kitchen. "From now on, we should call that curve on the Thornhollow grade 'Dick's corner.'

"Sounds good to me," I replied, smiling.

Tales From Working on a Dude Ranch

Richard V. Dalke

After lunch we went out and stabilized the bed of the truck with a set of chains, to be taken off only when we needed to use the hydraulic lift.

Richard V. Dalke

Chapter 7

Advice From a Travel Agent

Toward the end of my first summer on the ranch, I had to make a decision. Should I come back to the ranch the next season or do something different?

Many of the guests that came to the ranch first learned about the Bar M from Lee, a travel agent who had an office on Hollywood Boulevard in Los Angeles, California. He specialized in Dude Ranches and flew in his private single engine Cessna from ranch to ranch, much like a restaurant critic would eat meals at local cafés before writing a review.

The difference would be that Lee would always schedule his time with the different dude ranches before showing up. He would stay for a week or so, riding the horses, swimming in the pools, participating in the volleyball games and the square dances. He told me that the Bar M was his favorite dude ranch. He took pictures of the ranch and made slides from them. He would show these slides to potential clients at his travel agency, many of them becoming regular guests on the ranch. His advice was free to his clients; the dude ranches contracted with him for each client that became a guest that season. Mr. B was very generous with Lee, paying him an extra commission and filling his airplane with gas each time he came to visit.

The Bar M was known as an 'authentic dude ranch.' It was an actual working cattle ranch, old

Richard V. Dalke

fashioned and rustic. The ranch house and annex were both over 100 years old, guests made their own beds during the week, all meals were served in the dining room. Guests were expected to learn how to groom and saddle their own horses.

Guests that were seeking a spa type atmosphere with tennis courts, massage therapists, a bar with fancy drinks, a restaurant for meals, a wrangler that brought their horse to them saddled, bridled and ready to go would not feel comfortable on this guest ranch.

Lee liked the ruggedness of the Bar M and would suggest this type of ranch to the clients in Los Angeles that were seeking the 'real thing.'

Many of the guests that came to the Bar M became long term friends with the Bakers, returning year after year, with 2nd and 3rd generations of children growing up and coming to the ranch for their vacations as well. Hope found that guests that were friends or family members of previous guests often made the most satisfied visitors, since they knew exactly what to expect.

Toward the end of my first season on the ranch, I saw Lee sitting on the front porch in one of the rocking chairs.

"Do you think I should keep coming back to the ranch for a summer job?" I asked him.

"You're a young man, you'll have plenty of responsibilities when you get older. I would highly suggest you work here as many seasons as you want, have lots of fun, meet interesting people, enjoy the beautiful scenery and eat the wonderful food," he replied. "I wouldn't worry too much about how much money you're making. It's very hard to work at a job like this when you're older and married, with children, a mortgage and other responsibilities. Enjoy this adventure while you're young and healthy and you're able to."

Tales From Working on a Dude Ranch

Richard V. Dalke

I followed his advice and came back to work for two more seasons – working from March to September each year.

Richard V. Dalke

Chapter 8

Encountering Bees on a Hillside

Working on the ranch gave me a chance to learn about myself, face tough challenges, and experience a special sense of healing. A combination of the stunning Blue Mountain scenery, encounters with mountainside dangers, and trials of overcoming fear, created a special 'cocoon of intensity' that helped people break through their usual emotional barriers and share more deeply of themselves. This was true not

Tales From Working on a Dude Ranch

Richard V. Dalke

only for the guests, but for those of us that worked there as well. The setting, the challenges, the intensity made it possible for an older couple to heal their anxiety, a young woman to quickly heal from her allergy to bee stings, a group of shy guests to open up to one another and my brothers and I to experience a taste of grace under pressure.

I came to the Bar M dude ranch after my first year of college, nineteen years old, shy, awkward and unsure of myself. By the time the summer season was over, I felt like I'd grown up. It became easier for me to talk to girls, deal with hair-raising challenges, accept responsibility, and feel more confident in strenuous situations.

A typical week on the ranch would include: training horses, building trails, leading guests on rides, teaching square dance lessons, eating wonderful homemade cooking, going on an overnight pack trip, milking a cow by hand, hauling

Tales From Working on a Dude Ranch

Richard V. Dalke

hay and feeding the stock. If there was time, I'd also get to swim in the natural warm-springs swimming pool, well-known for its healing mineral waters.

But it was one of those out-of-the-ordinary encounters that helped me learn something special. One of those extraordinary moments started out as a normal Sunday afternoon. The guests arrived about 3:00 in the afternoon, were assigned their rooms, unpacked and eagerly waited for the clanging of the large bell. When the signal came, they sat down to a gigantic home-cooked meal of fried chicken, special Bar M salad, hand rolled bread and mashed potatoes with country gravy.

Our visitors that week included the usual mix of parents, children, professional people, experienced riders, and untested horsemen. Normally, guests were very talkative, especially those that had been at the ranch previously, eager to make new friends and reestablish former contacts.

Tales From Working on a Dude Ranch

Richard V. Dalke

This particular crowd, however, seemed quieter than usual. The large group, totaling fifty or more guests, contained only a few acquaintances who knew each other. As they sat around the tables in the main dining room they talked mostly to their own family members, the kitchen help and the hired ranch hands. They spoke with the other guests they didn't know haltingly, if at all.

After eating and a short rest, the children burst through the front door of the ranch house or their individual cabins, their parents a few steps behind, and headed directly for the feed bunks where the horses were tied up.

"I get the black one with the stripe on his face," yelled one excited rider. Another shrieked, "can I have the pinto?"

"We try to match the riders with the horses," Slim, an older wrangler, replied. "If you haven't ridden very much, we'll be sure to put you on a horse that hasn't got much experience either."

The kids looked at him with horror, not sure whether he was joking or not. Slim just grinned. The horses stood nonchalantly munching their hay, oblivious to the scrutinizing eyes looking them over. We assigned each guest their four-legged transportation for the week, a well-fitting saddle and the bridle that had been pre-selected for that particular mount. The other wranglers and I then helped them prepare for their first ride of the week.

Two of my brothers had also come down to the ranch that weekend to help. We planned to drive back to our home town after dinner and what we knew would be our last ride of the summer. We hadn't seen each other for five months and were eager to get reconnected.

Dan, who had been promoted to foreman, decided to split the guests into three groups. "Dick,"

Tales From Working on a Dude Ranch

Richard V. Dalke

he said, why don't you and your brothers take the 'veterans' up on the hill. I'll take one group with me down-river and Jerry can lead the others upriver to the big flat."

We guided roughly twenty-five subdued would-be-cowboys and cowgirls up-river, through the gate at Bear Creek and then uphill on the North Slope. This was my favorite part of the day. The tangy smell of saddle leather, the clip-clop of hooves on the road, the freshness of the mountain air energized me. I loved the feel of a strong, sure-footed horse under me, the sound of the river gurgling over smooth stones, the relaxing peace of the hillside. I was riding my favorite horse, an Appaloosa-Tennessee Walker mixed gelding named 'King.' As the lead wrangler, I was responsible for opening gates, making sure the guests were safe and allowing the horses to rest in suitable places. My brother Gene rode about ten horses behind me, in

Richard V. Dalke

the middle of the string. Eric, a more experienced horseman, rode at the tail end of the line, to close the gates and keep an eye on the less seasoned riders.

It was a breathtaking sight after we had navigated several switchbacks and climbed to a crest overlooking the Bar M. Looking down, the riders could see the Umatilla River, the ranch houses, the hot springs swimming pool and the rugged log barns. More than a few were nervous about looking over the edge.

Our primary concern that summer had been the yellow jacket nests, which were safe for three or four riders to amble past, but hazardous for five or more. The bees were merely aroused by the dust stirred up by the first few animals, after that, they swarmed out looking for blood. At the steepest point on the trail, overlooking a several hundred

Richard V. Dalke

foot drop-off to the river below, we ran into the yellow devils.

Pandemonium broke loose. The less skillful riders, not aware of what was happening or what to do, held their jittery mounts back, not letting them run out of the insects' way. Many of the horses were stung. Five wounded ponies with terrified riders clinging for dear life stampeded up the hill. Guests were screaming. A young bride, on her honeymoon, was stung over thirty times. "Oh my God," she wailed. "I'm allergic to yellow jackets. I'll swell up like a watermelon." She bailed out of her saddle, tore off her t-shirt and frantically tried to rub the bees off her skin and out of her hair. An older couple in their sixties, terrified of being stung, lost control and fell off their mares. They both got up and anxiously brushed the dust from their jeans, afraid to get back on. I was thankful they hadn't rolled down the hill or over the cliff.

Tales From Working on a Dude Ranch

Richard V. Dalke

Eric, eager to assist the others, raced his black gelding back and forth howling "get the hell out of there" and managed to pull a dozen or more riders out of the way of the yellow demons. Gene was able to help the remaining riders maintain control of their mounts.

I felt an unusual calmness, almost meditative. In other panic-stricken situations, I had felt overwhelmed and disoriented. I'd run back and forth, unable to make decisions, unable to lessen my fear. But this time, I had a sense of reassurance. I felt serene and in control. I rode King up ahead, dismounted, tied him to a bush and told the five or six riders behind me where to safely graze their horses. I then walked back, assisted the young honeymooner comb the bees out of her hair (her new husband had covered her with his shirt) and helped her relax. I put both of the older guests back

Richard V. Dalke

on their horses, tightened the cinch on their saddles and spoke soothingly to them.

"We'll take the shorter trail back down, so we're not in anymore danger," I said. "I think we've had enough excitement for our first ride." They both smiled and breathed a sigh of relief. I could see the anxiety melt out of their eyes.

Meanwhile my brothers had helped the other guests round up their now sedate steeds, remount and get ready for the trip back. I made a note to myself exactly where the yellow jackets nest was, so when we returned to the ranch house, I could let Jerry know where to apply the bee powder. We made the rest of the ride back down the hill without incident, though I knew my brothers and I would have a lot to talk about on the drive home that night. After tying up the horses and brushing them down, we went in for a late supper.

Tales From Working on a Dude Ranch

Richard V. Dalke

The riders in our group were all talking excitedly, getting to know one another, quickly becoming friends. Before the meal was over, a traumatic experience had become an icebreaker, giving them a chance to heal their shyness. The enthusiasm was so tangible that riders from the other groups were wishing they could have ridden with ours. The twenty year old honeymooner was cared for by a doctor who'd come for his two week vacation, then soaked in the warm springs swimming pool with her husband. She didn't need any further treatment. We were all surprised she hadn't become horribly ill.

"It's a day I'll never forget," she said. "I've never healed this fast from bee stings before. What a great story to tell the children we have someday." She smiled shyly at her young groom.

The older couple were complimentary as well. "You were so unruffled. You knew just what

Richard V. Dalke

to say to get us back on our horses. I never thought I'd ride again. I want to thank you."

It was hard for me to take the credit. I'd felt like guardian angels had been looking over my shoulder the entire time, helping me remain calm and decisive. I silently thanked them for letting me experience the healing power of their grace.

Chapter 9

Going on a Pack Trip

It was the middle of the week – we pretty much always left on Tuesdays or Wednesdays for the overnight pack trips, depending whether we were going on a one-nighter or a two-nighter. Only the hardiest of guests were usually up for the two-nighters, and we had several guests that week who fit the bill well. Enough guests had signed up for the longer pack trip and it was my turn to be the wrangler that went with Mr. B to help out.

Tales From Working on a Dude Ranch

Richard V. Dalke

Virginia was a lady who owned a summer cabin on the Umatilla River, right next to the ranch. Mr. B had sold several lots a short distance from the ranch house and swimming pool years earlier to bring in extra money during a slow year. She knew the horses and the trails and wasn't intimidated by the rigors of camping out. We also had a long-time guest, Jean, who had come almost every year for over 20 years. Usually when she came to the ranch for her two week vacation, she would take a lunch and go for long trail rides by herself, enjoying the solitude and peacefulness of the mountains. She was a welcome addition to our 2 day pack trip, an experienced horsewoman and pleasant company.

Several others were in their 20's and were good riders, having come to the ranch several times previously as well as owning their own horse back home. There were about a dozen of us altogether.

Tales From Working on a Dude Ranch

Richard V. Dalke

Mr. B had one of the guests pack the sourdough starter in her saddle bags, so it would stay warm. Most of us didn't want that job because of the incredible odor it gave off if the container lid accidently opened when you took it out of the saddlebag. Mr. B would take the starter out when we got to the campsite and have the same guest put the sealed bowl into her sleeping bag at night – again to keep it warm.

We got all of the pack trip guests ready to go, saddled up and cinches tightened. Since we were going on one of the longer trips, we headed up river, past the flat and continued on past the ranger station and onto the National Forest. Their trails were often better than ours, as they had professional equipment to build their trails with, while we plowed ours with a horse and a single-bottom plow.

Tales From Working on a Dude Ranch

Richard V. Dalke

We rode all morning, first along the river and then into the Blue Mountains, heading for the plateau on top.

We stopped for lunch along the way, tied up our horses to a tree and sat on the ground or tree stump or rock. From time to time when we got to a logging road, Mr. B would let us canter or gallop the horses for a short distance. This was one of the reasons that experienced guests liked to go on the pack trips, as this was pretty much the only time they would be allowed to let their horses go faster than a trot.

Later in the afternoon, we arrived at the campsite, and turned the horses loose. We put a bell on one or two of them that we knew would stay close to camp, so we'd be able to locate them in the morning. Sometimes they'd be a quarter mile away, usually not more than a mile.

Tales From Working on a Dude Ranch

Richard V. Dalke

Then we set up our tents, built a campfire and roasted marshmallows. Some of the guests liked to burn their marshmallows; I always liked to get mine toasted just right, almost to the point where it melted off the stick, toasted to a delicious golden brown. I'd pluck it into my mouth after letting it cool for a bit or place it on a graham cracker with Hershey's chocolate for a 'S'more.' Hmmm. Very tasty.

There wasn't quite enough room for me in any of the tents, so I put my sleeping bag close to the fire and slept under the stars. There was always something magical about sitting around the campfire, toasting marshmallows and telling stories that made us all share more of ourselves. Some of the guests would tell ghost stories, but often they were memorable family stories. We would talk about what we appreciated about each other, about nature, the horses, just being outdoors. The guests

Richard V. Dalke

would often open up, parents would listen to their children, teenagers would sit in rapt attention to their dad or mom, something many of them didn't experience often at home.

Early the next morning, I thought this would be my chance to really impress Mr. B and the guests. I got up just before dawn and headed for the ringing of the bells. I carried the bridle for my horse and a halter with a rope attached to it for leading one of the horses that had a bell around her neck. I was counting on the rest of the herd to follow us back toward camp. I was sure the guests would be surprised and pleased to have their horses close by, ready to saddle up first thing after breakfast.

I found them a little over a mile away, munching on the grass along the open hillside. I counted them – they were all there. I put my hand out to catch King with a 'horse goody' and put the bridle on him. I led him to one of the mares with a bell on, caught her and put the halter on. I jumped on King bareback and rounded up the others until they were all close together and started leading them back to camp. I was glad that the others followed us. We had to go through one gate, which meant I had to open the gate while leading another horse. Not an easy trick, but I managed to get it open, let the others through and close it again without losing any of the horses.

I rode into camp with all of the horses, proud of my accomplishment and eager to get the praise I thought I'd earned from the other campers and Mr. B.

Mr. B. looked at me and stated - "You should have left the horses out there. It's part of the two-night pack trip experience for the guests to learn how to catch their own horses and ride them without saddles back to the camp."

Tales From Working on a Dude Ranch

Richard V. Dalke

I felt foolish and embarrassed. Virginia came to my defense.

"Dick told me this was his first two-night camping trip, Howard – he was just trying to help us all out. I, for one, am glad he brought my horse in this morning. I didn't feel like riding bareback first thing this morning."

I appreciated what she had to say, but made sure I asked Mr. B what was expected of me after that.

The rest of the pack trip went well; all the guests enjoyed the long ride, but were a bit saddle sore and eager to relax in the swimming pool when we returned to the ranch.

Chapter 10

Square Dancing in the Barn

Each week, on Saturday night, we would go to the log barn which we called the Rec Barn, next to one of the corrals, walk up the stairs and get ready to have fun with round dancing and square dancing. Mr. B would put on the records and give us instructions. After dinner, each of us wranglers changed into a clean shirt, put on our best pair of jeans, our fancy cowboy hat, and shined up our boots. The girls that worked in the

Richard V. Dalke

kitchen would put on dresses and the guests would put on their dancing outfits as well.

It was often our favorite part of the week. We'd dose-e-doe, allemande left and right, swing that girl behind us and square dance for hours. Some of the dances were silly – we'd put our left foot in and our left foot out, do the hokey pokey and learn that that was what it was all about. There would be a few slow songs for those that were sweet on each other to dance together.

I loved dancing and was good at it; it was one of the times during the week that I became very popular, often sought out as a partner. When I asked a girl to dance, I was never turned down. Sometimes two or three girls would pursue me at the same time. It was so much different than my experience back home. Whenever I'd go out to a dance club or a nice hotel with a dance floor, I would often have to take that 'walk of shame' back

Tales From Working on a Dude Ranch

Richard V. Dalke

to my seat after a girl turned me down, not wanting to dance with me. Years later, I became an Arthur Murray dance instructor, recreating the fun and attractiveness I felt at the dances at the ranch.

There was very little drinking at the square dances, Mr. B was very religious and drinking was not allowed. From time to time, some of the guests would sneak a drink from a bottle of whiskey or have a few beers before they got there, but once the music started, we never saw any alcohol inside the dance hall. That was ok with me – I never was much of a drinker.

The barn had a few strange critters that came to visit from time to time – large rats that ran across the top of the log beams, bats that hung from the rafters. We avoided mentioning them when the guests were in the hall; we wanted the guests to have a good time dancing, not worrying about the creatures that sometimes inhabited the Rec barn.

Tales From Working on a Dude Ranch

Richard V. Dalke

But one Saturday evening, we encountered an unwelcome visitor that was too close to ignore. I had just done a dose-e-doe around my partner and then reached out to Dan's partner – a girl that he was sweet on – to start an allemande left when I noticed a large water beetle on her chest. I thought it might be one of those pieces of jewelry that some women liked to wear that are in the shape of bugs. This one was huge – probably 4 or 5 inches long with his feelers twitching back and forth.

I asked her "what is that?" pointing to the creature on her shirt. She looked at me puzzled at first and then looked down. She screamed and knocked the water beetle off her shirt and continued screaming for several more minutes. Dan went with her as she ran from the room, trying to calm her down.

A little later after the incident was over, Dan came back in and looked at me.

Tales From Working on a Dude Ranch

Richard V. Dalke

"Why didn't you just knock that big beetle off her instead of pointing at it?"

"First of all, I hate big bugs, they freak me out too. I had one land on my shoulder once when I was out in the hay field, mowing alfalfa. By the time I was done knocking that thing off my shirt, the path I'd woven through the field made the hay crop look like a disaster. They still give me the shivers. Second of all, I'm not about to touch your girlfriend's chest no matter what's on it," I replied.

He nodded, but we both knew the square dancing was over for that night.

The incident had spooked the other guests as well. We all went back to our rooms, and turned in for the night.

Chapter 11

Exhilaration on the North Slope

The Baker's primary source of income came from the guests who came during the summer and some special occasions like graduation ceremonies and corporate retreats. But they also kept about 35 head of cattle, most of them Herefords to add a little income during the winter months. It also made the Bar M a real ranch, with working cowboys.

Whenever we went up the hill to bring down the cattle or horses, we often had to ride off the

Richard V. Dalke

main trails that we took the guests on. We might have to ride on an old deer trail or no trail at all. The cattle would often hide where it was hard to get to them, in the brush or in a pocket of scrubby hillside trees with low hanging branches. We wanted to stay as safe as possible on the mountainside, but from time to time we needed to take a few chances to get the job done.

One afternoon, three of us went up on the north-slope to bring the cattle down, in order to check them for any health problems and to take the grown steers to market.

I was riding King, my favorite Appaloosa gelding. Not only did he look great, with a roan colored blanket of spots over his hindquarters, he also had a fast-paced shuffling walk that was comfortable to ride all day long.

He was also fearless. We were on a narrow trail on the mountainside. We'd rounded up all of the cows, steers and heifers and started them down the hill. Most of them were staying in line, coming down the trail as we wanted them to. About half way down, one ornery two year old heifer broke away and ran in the opposite direction, trying to escape back up the hill.

I tapped King and we took off at a full gallop, overtaking the young animal and forcing her to turn around. I realized that was a bit dangerous as we were on the side of the hill, staring down into a 200 foot canyon. But it was exhilarating! I'd rarely felt so alive. The last time I felt like that was driving my brother's sports car on a two lane highway and finally being able to pass a line of trucks and several cars all at the same time after following behind them for untold miles.

After we got all the cattle down the hill, through the gate and into the corral, Dan turned to me.

Tales From Working on a Dude Ranch

Richard V. Dalke

"You know, it would have been all right to let that one go, you were chasing that heifer at full speed on a pretty narrow trail. That hillside is very steep too."

I nodded. "Sometimes you just have to go with your gut. I knew King felt it too. He was very surefooted and eager to go. I'll be sure to be more careful next time."

I knew in my mind that it was one of those moments in life when I just had to go for it. Those moments didn't come that often and I knew I would remember it forever.

Chapter 12

Getting Bucked Off

The other wranglers and I always rode the horses that weren't ready for the guests. They were either too green, too mean, too untrained or too skittish. We made sure the guests – even the experienced riders – got horses that were trained to neck rein and were willing to go when and where a rider wanted them to.

One Sunday in late August, Mr. B was getting ready to lead a new group of guests on their first ride of the week. I was going to ride Bonita – a

Tales From Working on a Dude Ranch

Richard V. Dalke

two year old that was very green. She was also very skittish, and got nervous whenever she heard any sounds that seemed a little loud or out of the ordinary. She also didn't like anything touching her side – like tree branches or bushes that rubbed against her while going down the trail.

Mr. B had to twist her ear before I could get on the first time. It wasn't to hurt her, but to distract her from noticing a rider getting on her back. I climbed slowly into the saddle, swung my leg over and slipped my right foot into the stirrup, being careful not to touch her side. She jumped around a little bit, but settled down once she fell in line behind the other horses. She'd been born on the ranch, so was used to following the other horses on the mountainside trails. She quickly calmed down as soon as she returned to that routine.

I was the wrangler at the end of the line, as we headed up river to the big flat. We went past the

Tales From Working on a Dude Ranch

Richard V. Dalke

gates that led to Rock Creek and then to Bear Creek, staying on flat ground about a mile from the ranch.

When we got to the big flat – a meadow several acres in size, we stopped to let the horses eat. I was about to learn something new about Bonita.

I loosened the reins a bit, to let her munch on the sweet grass. I also relaxed in the saddle, glad to let go of the tension of paying close attention to her every move. The reins were just a bit too loose, and so was I. Bonita stepped on the edge of the rein, close to where it attached to the bit on her bridle. She freaked out, thinking her head was tied to the ground. She started bucking and stomping. Completely unprepared for what was happening, I fell off, getting struck several times by her hooves, my hat and glasses falling to the ground.

Tales From Working on a Dude Ranch

Richard V. Dalke

It was over in a matter of seconds. She'd stepped off the rein, so she no longer felt like she was tied down. She stood close by blowing wind out of her nostrils and shivering, obviously still frightened. I had managed to hang on to one of the reins, so she hadn't run away. I picked myself up, brushed off my pants, picked up my glasses and placed the now dilapidated straw hat back on my head.

I looked at the other riders. They were sitting on their mounts, wide-eyed and astonished. I wasn't mad at Bonita, she hadn't been mean – she was scared. I was embarrassed for not being prepared for whatever might happen when riding a green horse.

I calmed her down by stroking her neck, made sure the cinch hadn't come loose and clambered back on. I knew I had to follow that old cowboy rule of climbing back on the horse that

Tales From Working on a Dude Ranch

Richard V. Dalke

threw me, otherwise the other riders would feel uncomfortable trusting their horses as well. We let the horses eat a bit more and continued on with our ride.

I made sure to keep a closer eye on my reins when I was on Bonita or any of the other horses, never letting them get loose enough to be stepped on. We also knew to never tie her head to the ground or to one of her feet; an old horseman practice that Mr. B sometimes used on pack trips, to keep a horse from wandering too far from camp.

Richard V. Dalke

Chapter 13

Gas Can Incident

It was early in the spring, before the guests were scheduled to arrive for their summer vacations. Our job for the day was to work on building and repairing the trail on the south side of the river. On this day, Mr. B and I were heading up to the Eagle's nest trail, to drill blasting holes and jackhammer the rocks loose.

I was riding an older sway backed pinto, a gentle horse Mr. B had bought from a neighbor down the road. I was carrying a 5 gallon can of gas

Richard V. Dalke

for the Swedish-made jackhammer that Mr. B operated on the trail. He rode a large bay and pulled a pack horse carrying the jackhammer. I wasn't worried about getting bucked off, even though I was carrying a metal can that flopped around a bit.

We crossed the river and headed into what we called the stump farm. The meadow had gotten its name from the many trees that had been cut down in the past, providing lumber for the ranch. Just past the stump farm was the path leading up the side of the mountain, one we called the Eagle's nest trail. The Eagles had built their home near the top of a 100 foot tall Ponderosa Pine tree that stood close to the edge of the trail. I often touched the pine tree's jigsaw bark whenever we passed it on our trail rides. I felt like I was getting a blessing from nature, similar to the luck football players sought when they slapped their team symbol in the locker room just before a big game. The nest didn't seem to be inhabited any longer, but the name stuck.

We noticed that the trails were soft and muddy from the spring rains. About three quarters of a mile up the trail, after negotiating a half-dozen or so switchbacks, we turned one corner that was especially soft. My horse stepped on the edge of the trail with his hind foot and it gave way. We tumbled over backwards, somersaulting down to the trail below. It seemed to happen in slow motion. I fell off, lucky to avoid getting a saddle horn in my gut. My pony waited patiently for me on the trail below and I was surprised to see that I still held on to the gas can that I'd been carrying the entire way up the mountain.

Mr. B was about a quarter mile ahead on the trail. He stopped and asked – "you ok?"

"Yep, we're both ok. Soft trail, we went over backwards. No harm done to the gas can.

Tales From Working on a Dude Ranch

Richard V. Dalke

Didn't lose a drop," I replied, a bit shaken up. I got back on my horse and we continued up the mountainside, ready to continue our work for the day. We made a note of the spot in the trail that had given way, so we could come back later and repair it. Future repairs would require digging out the hillside and placing medium-sized rocks along the edge. The digging would make the trail wider and the rocks would force the horses to stay on the inside of the path, next to the hillside. These repairs would help the trail last longer and help the guests remain safe during the trail rides.

Chapter 14

Getting Lost in the Mountains

It was midweek – time to take out the pack trip to the top of the North Slope – ending up close to a camping spot near the small town of Tollgate. When the guests were interested in signing up for the overnight pack trip – and often they were – Mr. B would allow one of the wranglers to go with him to help out. We took turns, so each week a different wrangler would get a chance to go camping.

Tales From Working on a Dude Ranch

Richard V. Dalke

Dan brought the sleeping bags, food, tents and extra gear in the truck. The trip by road was over 50 miles – our ride was only a few miles up to the top of the mountain and a few miles more along the trails to our camping spot.

This week was my turn to be the wrangler on the pack trip – my first one-nighter. I added a lasso to the front of my saddle and strapped on the hunting knife I'd gotten from my dad. It was mostly for show, but I thought it might come in handy. I'd been on plenty of trail rides, but never to the top of the mountain. I looked forward to seeing some new territory. I rode at the tail end, closing the gates we went through and keeping an eye on the riders that were close to me.

After breakfast, the riders came out to the feed bunks where the horses stood, munching on the grass hay, eager to begin. The more experienced riders would brush down their horses and saddle

Richard V. Dalke

them without a wrangler's help. We helped the inexperienced and younger horsemen get ready.

Once we were saddled up, Mr. B stopped his horse and turned to face the group.

"Keep a little distance from the horse in front of you so you don't get kicked, but not so far away that you can't see 'em. We don't want anyone getting lost," he admonished. "Be sure to stay on the trail, too. We don't want anyone falling off their horse. Ok, let's head on up the mountain, daylight's burnin'."

I saw to it that any stragglers were mounted and ready to go. There were always last minute cinches to be tightened and ponies that were more interested in chomping on the hay in the feed bunks than starting their work for the day.

When everyone was ready, we followed Mr. B down the road, through the gate at Rock Creek and headed up the mountain, riding back and forth

Tales From Working on a Dude Ranch

Richard V. Dalke

along the switchbacks. The higher we got, the greater the view – we could see the entire ranch – the cabins, the ranch house, the annex, the swimming pool, the river below. It was spectacular.

We rested when we got to the top of the hill, tightening up any cinches that had loosened up a bit, and made sure the riders were feeling comfortable. We let the horses rest and eat the fresh grass. The horses were always more willing to go on trips like this when they got a chance to eat the wild cucumber and fresh pasture grass that they couldn't get down at the feed bunks.

After a few minutes, Mr. B hollered at us, "Time to go."

I helped a few riders climb back on their horses. A short distance later, we went through the gate at the top of the mountain, which separated the Bar M Ranch from the Forest Service land. We'd gone a mile or so down a Forest Service path when

Tales From Working on a Dude Ranch

Richard V. Dalke

Mr. B headed off the trail – taking a short cut through the woods. A young boy had gotten too far behind the rider in front of him and became confused and started crying. I rode up ahead to see what the problem was and realized we were all in trouble. I couldn't see the other riders or where they'd gone. There wasn't a trail, and the ground was covered with pine needles, so there weren't any tracks to follow. I had no idea where to go – the 6 riders that were left behind were all depending on me to catch up with the other riders who had ridden ahead without us.

I prayed silently for any kind of guidance I could get to help us out of this predicament.

Becky – a college aged girl that I had been talking to during the week was in our group – ready and willing to help, even though she didn't know the trail either. She was able to calm the riders down and let them know they were in good hands

Tales From Working on a Dude Ranch

Richard V. Dalke

with the experienced wrangler that would keep them safe. I knew there were cougars, bears, rattle snakes and bees on that mountain and it was my job to keep everyone unharmed while we found the rest of the group.

I gathered the seven of us together, which included me, Becky, a teenager, another adult and three other young riders. Rather than trying to find the rest of the group by riding through the brush and off the trail, I decided to stay on the Forest Service trail and hoped to find a logging road that led to a main road or highway. The trail soon came to an old dirt road that had posts with numbers on them. The guests stayed close as we headed north, being careful not to lose sight of the rider in front of them. I noticed that the numbers on each post were getting progressively smaller. I hoped that meant we were heading closer to a highway or main Forest Service road.

Tales From Working on a Dude Ranch

Richard V. Dalke

Becky rode up beside me and asked, "do you know where you're going?"

"No, but don't tell the others that. We all need to stay calm and hope for the best."

I didn't tell her about the wild animals that were known to live on this part of the mountain. We rode for over an hour, the sun getting hotter, the responsibility for the safety of the guests weighing heavy on my shoulders. When we came to forks in the road, I made sure we always chose the trail that had posts with diminishing numbers on them. Eventually we came to a wider road, one that looked like it might lead somewhere.

After another half-hour or so, we came to the main highway and I saw a gas station a short distance away. I drew the riders together.

"We need to stay close together here, and ride in single file alongside the highway, so the cars will have plenty of space to us pass by."

Tales From Working on a Dude Ranch

Richard V. Dalke

I had Becky ride at the end to keep an eye on the younger riders. When it was safe, we rode across the highway and up to the gas station.

Parked just to the right of the gas pumps was the Bar M truck loaded with all the gear along with a dark bay horse. Dan came out of the gas station restroom and was very surprised to see us.

"What are you guys doing here?" he asked.

I told him what had happened – how we had gotten disconnected from the rest of the group. He cussed Mr. B under his breath, knowing he had a habit of taking off through the brush without warning, assuming the other riders would follow close behind.

He pointed down the road. "Just follow the highway about three quarters of a mile then turn left onto the dirt road past the old barn. The rest of the riders should be about a quarter mile up the dirt road – that's where we always stop for lunch when

Richard V. Dalke

we go on this packtrip. You guys are really lucky that I just happened to stop at the gas station. There'd be no way you'd have known where to go, since you've never been up here before. I'm going to pick up a couple of things and then drive the truck the rest of the way to the camp."

I thanked him for the directions and silently thanked my guardian angels for helping us get to the station at just the right time to meet with Dan.

We rode alongside the highway, turned at the old barn and found the other riders sitting on the rocks or nearby logs, eating their lunch.

"I always knew Dick would find the way," stated Mr. B to the others. "He's a great wrangler."

I bit my tongue, as I didn't want the riders to know just how scared I'd been and how close we'd come to facing a potential disaster. I looked over at Becky and could tell she understood what I was thinking. The seven of us got off our horses, tied

Richard V. Dalke

them up and joined the others for lunch, thankful to be out of danger.

I grabbed a sandwich, a couple helpings of potato salad, a bottle of pop and a can of beans. I'd forgotten to bring any eating utensils with me, so I used my hunting knife to eat the beans and potato salad.

One of the other campers saw me and thought that scene would make an interesting photograph. She got out her camera and snapped the picture. She sent a copy of it to me later.

That picture is still in my photo album. It's one of my brother's favorites, as I look like a real old-fashioned cowboy, straw cowboy hat on my head and mouth full of beans, eating off my dad's hunting knife.

Chapter 15

The Game Room

Just off the dining room in the main ranch house was the game room. It held a ping pong table and several smaller tables, often with unfinished jigsaw puzzles on them and cupboards full of games.

Sally was the undisputed jigsaw puzzle champion, able to put a puzzle together in record time. One summer we decided to have a competition, splitting up the guests who liked to do jigsaw puzzles into two groups. Sally's group and

Tales From Working on a Dude Ranch

Richard V. Dalke

Dick's group. I loved doing jigsaw puzzles, but it had been years since I'd put one together. I'd get into a groove, looking at what kind of piece the puzzle needed. I'd say to myself things like, "two pointy things on the top and bottom and two indents on the sides with blue sky on top and part of a tree branch on the bottom." I would scan all the pieces until I found just the right one to match what I was looking for and place it in the puzzle. Within minutes, both Sally and I could find dozens of pieces that fit. The other puzzle group members would stare in amazement.

Hope – Sally's mom – had set up two tables, each with the pieces of comparable 1000 piece jigsaw puzzles. The kitchen help, which included Sally, got afternoons off when they were done cleaning up after lunch. The guests of course could work on the puzzles at their leisure. Sally would work on her team's puzzle during the afternoons. I

95

Richard V. Dalke

went back to work after lunch with the horses or hauling hay or any number of other chores that needed to be done outside.

My team labored away on the puzzle in the morning and afternoons, and I worked on it after hours or during the few minutes I had before lunch. Within a few days both teams were close to finishing their puzzles. With only a few hundred pieces left in each one, each team tried to get as much done as possible. Normally we went to bed around 9pm, since we had to get up early to start the day. That night, I stayed up until almost midnight, putting in the last of the pieces and finishing our team's puzzle. In the morning, the other team claimed "no fair, you must have stayed up late to finish your puzzle."

"I guess my competitive nature must have come out. I just wanted to finish putting in the last few pieces." I said, smiling.

Tales From Working on a Dude Ranch

Richard V. Dalke

Hope would then shellac each of the puzzles and put them up on the wall like pictures, so the guests could enjoy what they had accomplished.

I also enjoyed playing ping pong. I would play Jerry or Dan, sometimes Tom, the youngest. I had a special paddle, shaped more like a pentagon than the usual oval shape and layered with soft rubber, rather than the dimpled rubber on most paddles. I'd played quite a bit in college – though the players I played there were much better than I was.

On the ranch I enjoyed teaching the young guests what I'd learned and showed a few how to hold the paddle and other techniques that improved their game. I remember one guest surprised to see a young boy improve his technique in a few minutes after just one short lesson. She thought I was some kind of master teacher or something.

Tales From Working on a Dude Ranch

Richard V. Dalke

"No, I just helped him see that turning his paddle a certain way could help him control the ball better," I replied. I later found out from the boy's mother that the young boy thought of me as someone he wanted to be like when he grew up. What a great compliment! I once had a baby pig named after me, but never a compliment like this!

Sally and I would also play 'Battleship' and Backgammon and a card game called 'war' as well as other games. She would often beat me – and was considered the champion game player on the ranch. After a while I developed a strategy for playing 'Battleship' and would win from time to time. She would be surprised, having almost never lost to any of the guests or family members.

"You're still the champ," I told Sally. "You win more often than I do." She looked up at the jigsaw puzzles on the wall and shook her head, recalling the puzzle contest from earlier that season.

Richard V. Dalke

Chapter 16

A Cow Named Integration

One summer, Mr. B bought a Holstein cow, so we could have fresh milk for the ranch. She was colored the usual white with black markings, standard for that breed of dairy cow. Wanting to show the guests that we were aware of world events, I thought a good name for her would be integration – since her coloring was an integration of black and white together.

The Bar M didn't have a milking barn like the dairy farm I'd lived on as a teenager. No stanchions, no bulk tank to cool the milk in or pneumatic milking machines to make the chore easier. We would have to milk Integration by hand.

We tied her to the manger in the lower part of the Rec barn, pulled up a three legged stool and did our best to fill up the 5 gallon stainless steel pail.

Gene did most of the milking at first since he had strong forearms from shoeing the horses. My biceps were in pretty good shape from hauling hay and building trail, but I had a hard time getting more than a few squeezes of milk out of her before I had to pause. Both Dan and I eventually took over the milking duties, as Gene was busy with both the cooking and the horseshoeing.

The cats loved to come around and get a stream of fresh milk squirted in their direction. We'd laugh when the kittens got milk sprayed all over their faces. They'd just lick it off themselves and each other, happy for the warm meal.

Integration rarely kicked, even when we turned her teats sideways to squirt the cats and I was glad she was so good natured. I had often gotten kicked when I worked on my granddad's dairy farm, so I was pleasantly surprised to see that our black and white cow could be so gentle. I would tell the guests that she was a good example of how integration could really work!

Richard V. Dalke

Chapter 17

Designing a Sundial

The trail rides and pack trips always started at set times during the day. The guests would often come out asking what time it was, as many of them didn't have watches or didn't want to wear them while riding the horses.

I came up with the idea of turning a large stump near the tack room into a Sundial, so anyone coming out to ride the horses could tell the time.

I found a steel rod and pounded it into the top of the stump. The stump stood about 5 feet tall,

Tales From Working on a Dude Ranch

so I placed the rod so it would rise up about one foot out of the top. In that way, no matter where the sun was, a shadow could be seen on the ground any time during daylight hours. Over a period of several days, I'd try to stay close to the stump at the top of each hour. I had cut out 15 small pieces of cardboard, with hours written on each one for each sunlit hour – from 6am to 9pm. I nailed each one into the ground at the tip of the shadow indicating the time. The pieces of cardboard were placed progressively closer to the stump as the time got closer to noon and then placed farther away as the afternoon shadows got longer. I had to take into consideration that it was daylight savings time during the summer months, so the shortest shadow was off by an hour from the true time. By the time the sun went down, the placement of the cardboard pieces looked more like an ellipse than a circle.

Tales From Working on a Dude Ranch

Richard V. Dalke

"What the heck are you doing?" Dan asked, seeing me run outside at the stroke of noon while we were eating lunch.

"I've always loved sundials," I replied – "nature's way of telling time. So I'm making one – using that old stump next to the tack room as the center of the sundial."

Dan just shook his head. Another one of Dick's crazy ideas, I'm sure he was thinking.

We used it for the rest of that season. A little science lesson for the young guests to appreciate, a way to know the time of day for those that didn't wear a watch.

The homemade sundial didn't survive the winter, the cardboard pieces either blew away or withered away from the snow, wind and rain.

It's been 40 odd years since then and I still love sundials – it makes feel connected to the

Richard V. Dalke

rhythms of nature and to the universe. I plan to put one in my backyard this year or next.

Richard V. Dalke

Chapter 18

Rodeo Grounds/Swimming Hole

Every year at the ranch, we always had return guests and experienced riders that wanted to go to the rodeo grounds and the swimming hole before the week was over. We rarely rode the horses to either early in the week, as we wanted to be sure the guests had a chance to feel comfortable with their mounts, whether they were riding the same one they had in previous seasons or if they needed to get acquainted with a new one.

Tales From Working on a Dude Ranch

Richard V. Dalke

But by the end of the week, we often took a few of the experienced riders down river and across the Umatilla to the rodeo grounds. The Bakers had named it this way, because it was a flat meadow a hundred yards or so long and 50 yards wide – plenty of room to gallop or run the horses in. We'd only let a couple of riders at a time go at a full gallop down the length of the field. Most of them would stay in the saddle, more than once a few would bite the dust, but still eager to try it again. Rarely would the horses buck the guests off, more often it was a matter of coming to a quick stop or brushing underneath a tree branch at the end of the field. Sometimes riders simply urged their horses to run too fast for the level of experience they'd achieved.

Every once in a while, when we got off to rest the horses, we would look for four leaf clovers in the meadow. We learned that if you got really lucky, you could find not only 4 leaf clovers, but 5,

Tales From Working on a Dude Ranch

Richard V. Dalke

6 and even 7 leaf clovers. One year, Dan and I started collecting them. We ended up with 20 or so, and placed them inside a book to flatten them out, so they would be preserved for years. I no longer have my collection; I'm not sure if Dan does or not.

The swimming hole was not for people to swim in – it was for the horses to swim in – with riders on their backs. When the weather got really hot – in the 90's or 100's, the riders who felt comfortable riding bareback would head for the swimming hole with one of the wranglers. It was maybe 20 feet across, deep enough so the horses couldn't touch the bottom which forced them to swim across to shallower waters. It was a great way for guests and horses to cool down on a hot day. We usually took the same horses – the ones we knew loved the cool river water.

We advised riders to wear their tennis shoes, in case they needed to walk on the slippery river

Tales From Working on a Dude Ranch

Richard V. Dalke

rocks. I remember one incident when we had a rider who didn't know how to swim, fall off her horse and into the cold water. She panicked for a second, then thinking quickly, grabbed the tail of her horse, who swam across the swimming hole, pulling her with him. The horsed paddled toward a shallow area of the river, the rider close behind. When they got to the riverbank, we helped her climb back on her horse, thankful she was safe and unhurt.

She decided not to take her horse to the swimming hole the rest of that week, but remained thankful she had a great story to tell her friends when she returned home from her summer vacation.

Richard V. Dalke

Chapter 19

Parade Day

It was the end of my 1st year of working on the dude ranch. It was early September, time for the annual Pendleton Roundup, Happy Canyon and Parade. The Happy Canyon part of the festivities was a celebration of the heritage of the Native Americans who lived in the area, from the Umatilla Indian Reservation and surrounding tribes.

Mr. B saw this as a time to let the local folks know about the Bar M, in case some of them might

Tales From Working on a Dude Ranch

Richard V. Dalke

want to become guests at the ranch. His way of advertising was to have several of us ride in the Pendleton Roundup parade.

Slim suggested I ride Nugget, a gentle well-mannered sorrel gelding who was 5 or 6 years old. I felt a little disappointed, as I considered myself a good rider by then, having ridden for 6 or more hours a day all summer long. I'd been bucked off a time or two, and learned how to control the young horses that the guests couldn't handle.

The day before the parade, I picked out my favorite saddle, rubbed saddle soap into the leather, and polished the hardware, which brought out the sheen in the leather, and made the buckles and conchos shimmer. I liked that saddle, not only because it fit me perfectly, but because it looked great, with a double cinch, fancy leatherwork, tapaderos on the stirrups and embossed saddle bags. I tied my rope to the front of the saddle and found a good looking breast collar to complete the look I was going for.

On the day of the parade I caught Nugget, brought him down to the feed bunks and placed the freshly polished saddle on his back. We wanted the horses saddled up before we put them in the truck, so they'd be ready to go when we unloaded them in Pendleton.

We took the horses down to the loading chute next to the barn and loaded them into the truck. We checked to make sure the necessary chains for the bed were in place. No more tip overs! Mr. B drove the large Chevy truck with the horses loaded in the back, Slim followed with Smokey, a tall roan gelding that stood over 16 hands, loaded into the bed of his Toyota pickup. One of the guests and I rode in the cab of the Blue Chevy truck with Mr. B as he drove the 33 miles into town. When we got there, we unloaded our mounts close to the end

Richard V. Dalke

of the parade route. We tightened up our cinches, put the bridles on our horses and swung into our saddles.

Mr. B found out where we were supposed to be in the lineup of the parade. We rode behind a marching band and in front of a military float. Slim suggested we stay back a good distance from the band as the horses might get too excited from the noise and confusion.

Nugget perked up his ears. There was not only a lot of noise and excitement, there was the possibility of total mayhem from the Native American kids running under the horse's feet, picking up the quarters, dimes and nickels that spectators would throw into the streets. Nugget got nervous, prancing around and whinnying. I was thankful for Slim's advice and for picking out Nugget for me to ride. He was plenty for me to handle. Any of the other horses that I'd wanted to ride would have been out of control, spinning around and stepping on the little kids under their feet.

The next year, when it came time to ride in the parade, I rode King, a more spirited pony than Nugget, but by then I was a more experienced rider and knew what to expect.

By the end of my third season at the ranch, I decided to go on a date rather than ride in the parade. I had become more relaxed around the guests and more confident with the girls I met.

Two sisters had come from Southern California, one a year older than me, the other a year or two younger. On Friday night, several of the guests wanted to go into town to see the parade.

I'd been in the parade a couple of times, so I wasn't interested in watching the floats and bands, but I thought it might be nice to go on a date. I

Richard V. Dalke

asked Kendis, the older sister to come to a movie with me. She was happy to oblige.

We went into Pendleton and since we were a half hour early, we decided to stop at a little café to get a cup of coffee and a slice of pie. I didn't pay much attention to the other customers, but did notice a few of them looking us over. We ate our pie and drank our coffee, then went to the show. Afterwards, we drove back to the ranch and told the Bakers where we'd gone.

"What restaurant did you go to again," Gene asked, with an incredulous look on his face. I described it the best I could and he shook his head.

"You're really lucky, that place is known to be dangerous. There was a murder there just a few days ago – I'd never go in there myself. That's a really rough part of town."

Kendis opened her eyes wide – "I knew I came to the ranch to have some adventure in my life, but I didn't know we were close to having an adventure that I'd never forget."

Richard V. Dalke

Chapter 20

Freezing Rain

It was the middle of September, after most of the guests had gone home, but one middle aged couple – John and Marie – had remained to enjoy the peace and quiet, and were staying in the ranch house.

My home for the summer was a small whitewashed clapboard cabin we called the bunk house. It had been built in the 1930's as a cabin for the guests who came for the day to swim in the warm-springs swimming pool. The bunk house was

Tales From Working on a Dude Ranch

Richard V. Dalke

nestled in the trees about 100 yards north of the ranch house. It didn't have any heat or plumbing, only a lopsided outhouse out back that hadn't been used in years. When I got out of bed that fall morning, I saw snow on the ground. I usually walked across the grass to the bathroom in the Annex in my bare feet, but that day I pulled on my boots.

I showered and then returned to the cabin to get dressed for breakfast. After eating, we went outside to start the work day. Mr. B came up to the wranglers.

"Who's wanting to help me take the horses up Bear Creek to the top of the mountain? The grass is getting short down here on the hillside – we need to send them up through the gate on top, where there's more feed for them," he asked. "I know its cold out there, we'll stop at the little trailer to warm up when we get to the top."

Tales From Working on a Dude Ranch

Richard V. Dalke

No one else said anything, so I volunteered. John stated that he would like to join us, but wondered if there was some other way of getting to the top of the mountain other than riding in the cold. Mr. B gave him directions to the trailer by road, a drive of about 35 miles on the highway and a couple more miles on logging roads. We figured he'd get there before we could, so he could meet us at the top and open up the trailer. He also volunteered to bring the lunch – and to get a fire going in the little camp stove inside the trailer.

That sounded like a good idea to us, so we went to the barn to get our horses ready. I put on a pair of thick cotton socks, my long johns and a long sleeve shirt and coat. Over that I put on a slicker to cast off the rain. I noticed that Mr. B had on a pair of rubber galoshes over his boots. I didn't have a pair, so hoped my feet would stay warm and dry enough in my leather cowboy boots.

Tales From Working on a Dude Ranch

Richard V. Dalke

It was drizzling when we headed down the road and through the gate at Bear Creek, but it soon turned to sleet and freezing rain. My chest and arms felt warm enough, but my legs and feet were getting colder and colder. I soon learned that wet denim jeans and soaked cotton socks – no matter how thick – will not keep drenched legs or cold feet warm.

We drove the horses up the slope, pushing them further and further up the steep mountainside, often with only a deer trail to follow. From time to time, one or two of the horses would rebel, running along the hillside, trying to head back down the hill. I'd race up ahead and get them back in line, all the while swearing under my breath at the wayward horse and the pelting slush biting into my face.

After several hours, we made it through the gate, leading all of the horses onto the fresh pasture. We still had another mile or so of riding before reaching the trailer and what we hoped would be a warm camp stove.

I shuddered in the saddle, trying to hold as much warmth in my body as possible, avoiding numbness in my feet by pressing down on the stirrups. I tried to keep my hands warm by taking my gloves off from time to time, wringing out the rain and pulling them back on.

I was never more glad to see that little trailer house, even though it was tiny and obviously very weather-worn. But there was no car in sight.

"John hasn't gotten here yet. I hope he didn't get lost." Mr. B exclaimed. "We'll have to build our own fire. I'll open up the trailer, go ahead and see if you can find any dry wood in that little shed over there."

He pointed to a ramshackle lean-to a short distance away. We tied up our horses and I picked up a few dry sticks of wood and some shavings we could use for kindling and took them to the small mobile home. Mr. B unlocked the door and we went inside. After brushing off the ½ inch of dust from the table and stove top, Mr. B found a little newspaper, and put it and the kindling into the stove and lit the fire. A few minutes later, I took off my gloves and boots. My feet were purple. I wrung out my socks and my gloves and hung them close to the stove to dry out.

We heard a car pull up outside. Mr. B opened the door and let John in.

Our guest spoke. "Sorry I'm late. I took a wrong turn and went down the wrong logging road. It took me a while to find the way here. Here's lunch." He handed the sack to Mr. B and came inside, shutting the door behind him. He looked at me attempting to warm up my feet and spoke again.

"I was outside complaining about the weather, because I had to go out in the rain to open

Tales From Working on a Dude Ranch

Richard V. Dalke

up the gate to get here. Dick is sitting here with purple feet and he isn't saying a word, after riding for hours in the freezing rain. I don't think I'll ever complain again. I would make the suggestion to wear wool socks in the future, however," glancing at the pair of cotton socks drying near the stove.

"I can't stand the feel of wool against my skin," I muttered in defense.

Years later, I found just what I needed at a local Costco store. A pair of socks with a wool/cotton blend that felt good against my skin and kept my feet warm at the same time! I bought a dozen pair and I make sure to wear them whenever the weather turns the least bit nasty.

Richard V. Dalke

Chapter 21

Losing My Virginity

I was 25 years old and had returned to the ranch to help out for a couple of weeks. I'd worked at the ranch for 3 seasons and felt more comfortable around young women, but felt embarrassed that I was still a virgin. I knew that I was ok looking, but no Robert Redford. I had kept in good shape from the physical work on different ranches and hoped some girl would find me attractive. I was a little less shy, but still felt awkward around girls, especially in a romantic way.

Tales From Working on a Dude Ranch

Richard V. Dalke

It was Sunday afternoon and a new group of guests had just arrived. Most of the time folks came with their families; very few young women came by themselves. This week we had one guest from the east coast – an attractive woman with dark curly brown hair that hung down to the middle of her back and dark eyes that shone with eagerness and adventure. She was a few years older than me and I was pretty sure she was more experienced romantically than I was.

She spent time talking to me – asking me questions about the horses, riding near me during the morning and afternoon horseback rides, telling me about her life in New York.

I was flattered, but didn't really expect anything more, as her life was so much different from mine. As we spent more time together, I could tell she was interested in me. Even though I spent most of the year living in a mid-sized city, I think

Tales From Working on a Dude Ranch

Richard V. Dalke

she saw me as a "real cowboy." I certainly looked the part, with my boots, jeans and large straw hat. I figured she probably didn't see too many ranch hands where she was from.

Later in the week, we met at the pool. It was after dark, the stars were shining overhead and the warm water was steaming from the hot springs. We went in to the changing room to put on our bathing suits, came out and dove into the pool, the healing water washing away all of the tension and sore muscles from the day. She swam up to me in the pool and gave me a kiss. I wasn't expecting it, so I felt a little unnerved, but excited about what the evening might hold.

We swam and talked and kissed several more times, before deciding to get out of the pool. We dried off, changed back into our regular clothes and headed across the bridge. She took my hand and invited me to her room in the ranch house. It was

Tales From Working on a Dude Ranch

Richard V. Dalke

late, close to midnight – the other guests were in bed. I knew I would have to get up early in the morning to bring in the horses, but I didn't care.

I took off my boots before heading up the stairs as I didn't want to wake up the other guests clomping down the hallway in the middle of the night. We went up to the second floor and I followed her into her room. As we slowly undressed each other, I hoped she wouldn't be able to tell that this was my first time.

She had full and well developed breasts, a smooth flat tummy and full inviting lips. She struggled to pull my underwear over the bulge indicating my excitement.

We pulled the blankets aside and got under the sheets. I kissed her and she laid me on the bed. After letting let me know she was on the pill, she told me she liked being on top. I wasn't going to argue. She touched me and guided me into her, moving her hips up and down, slowly increasing the pace. I caressed her breasts, her tummy, her bottom, whatever I could reach. I was delirious with excitement. She moved faster, sliding me further inside her. I moved my hips to match hers. I exploded inside her within a couple of minutes, a decade of desire fueling my passion.

I held her for a few moments and we enjoyed exploring each other's body. Within a few minutes I was ready to go again. This time, I rolled her over and tenderly spread her legs. I slid gently into her, my excitement growing again. I controlled the pace this time, kissing her mouth, her nipples, her eyes. I started slowly, moving deeper and deeper inside her. When I couldn't stand it any longer, I plunged inside her as far as I could go and came a second time. She moaned as we collapsed together. God that felt good!

Tales From Working on a Dude Ranch

Richard V. Dalke

We talked for a while before she told me I needed to go – she didn't want other guests seeing me leave her bedroom. I slipped out of her room, closing the door quietly. I waited until I was downstairs before I put my boots back on, stepped through the front door and walked to my cabin, feeling like a new man. I was no longer a virgin!

We had several more nights that were similar, but when we said goodbye at the end of the week, we knew we wouldn't stay in touch. Our lives were just too different. Even so, I was very grateful for the gift she had given me.

Chapter 22

"Don't Cut Off Their Legs"

It was late in the summer, 5 or 6 of us were going on an overnight pack trip with Mr. B. This time we were hauling the horses the first 50 miles or so and then riding them the last few miles to our campsite. The plan was for Mr. B to drive the truck load of horses; Jean and I would follow behind in the blue Chevy pickup with the saddles, chainsaw, tents, food and other gear needed for a pack trip that would last several days. I made sure to strap my hunting knife to my hip. Never knew how it might come in handy.

Tales From Working on a Dude Ranch

Richard V. Dalke

Mr. B had a friend from a nearby town with
him in the truck. She'd driven up in her Cadillac
that morning and parked next to the ranch house.
She was a lady we'd never seen before and didn't
know much about, except the conclusions we came
to by noticing the outfit she was wearing. She
looked like she'd just come out of a JC Penney
catalog. Brand new boots, a cotton scarf tied around
her neck, new jeans tucked into her boots, denim
vest and a straw cowgirl hat. It was all brand new.
Not a scuff or worn spot on any of it. We could tell
she chose her outfit from pictures she'd seen of
cowgirls in a magazine.

Slim and I were loading up the pickup with
the gear, when he noticed her heading toward us
from the ranch house. We stood next to the pickup,
which was parked near the tack shed.

"I don't think she's ever been on a horse
before, much less gone on a pack trip," Slim

muttered under his breath, looking her up and down, spitting his tobacco on the ground.

When she got closer, I reached out to welcome her.

"Hi, my name's Dick, I'm one of the wranglers here. Jean and I will be following behind you and Mr. B in the pickup. Glad to meet you." I shook her hand.

"I've never gone on a trip like this before," she replied. Howard asked me to come along. I thought it might be fun."

"All of the other guests going on this trip are experienced riders. So we'll keep an eye out for you, in case you need any help." I offered.

She smiled and Mr. B came driving up with the truck and motioned for her to get in. She did so while Slim and I finished tying down the tarp to cover our load. Jean was already in the front seat of

Richard V. Dalke

the pickup. I climbed into the driver's side and started the engine.

"I filled up the gas tank last night, so we're ready to go," I told her.

Jean was a lady who'd been to the ranch many times – every year for the past 25 years or so and knew all of the trails and was a very experienced rider and camper.

We pulled out of the long driveway, past the Bar M sign at the entrance to the ranch and onto the road. We turned right at Thornhollow and headed up the grade. I pointed out Dick's corner to Jean and told her the story of how it got its name.

A few miles further, we turned onto the main highway and headed northeast trying to stay within visual distance of the truck load of horses.

After driving for about a half hour, Mr. B turned east onto a narrow 2 lane highway and we headed deeper into the mountains. From time to

Richard V. Dalke

time a logging truck would pass us - going toward town to unload the logs at the local lumber yard.

"This sure is a narrow highway," I mentioned to Jean, "and no shoulder to speak of either. Lots of blind curves, some of these truckers seem to be driving pretty fast and not always on their side of the road. I wouldn't want to end up in the ditch. I don't need any other corners named after me."

Mr. B had pulled ahead of us a bit, around a curve and out of sight. I drove as fast as I thought was safe on the narrow highway. It wasn't five minutes after I'd made the statement about ending up in the ditch, when we saw Mr. B standing next to the overturned truck. It was tipped over at a 45° angle alongside the edge of the highway in the ditch, the horses in the back scrambling to get their footing.

Tales From Working on a Dude Ranch

Richard V. Dalke

Jean gasped, "My God, you just talked about not wanting this to happen."

I nodded to Jean and stopped the pickup close to where the accident had happened. I scrambled out and ran up to Mr. B who was untying a few of the horses from the truck rack. Several had fallen which stretched their rope too tight to untie. The ropes would need to be cut off.

"What happened?" I asked.

"Damn trucker," replied Mr. B, "came around the curve too fast, driving on our side of the road. The only way I could avoid getting run over was to head for the ditch. Get me the chainsaw."

I pulled the chainsaw out of the back of the pickup and handed it to Mr. B.

Just then, Mr. B's female friend came around the end of the truck, noticed the chain saw in his hand and screamed.

Tales From Working on a Dude Ranch

Richard V. Dalke

"Oh, Howard, please don't cut off their legs."

Mr. B looked at her like she was crazy. He shouted back, "the chain saw is to cut the boards on the truck rack, so we can free the horses and get them unstuck. We need to get them off the truck, so we can get the truck out of the ditch and back on the road. We're not sawing any of their legs off."

Jean and I looked at each other and shook our heads.

As Mr. B freed their legs by cutting the lower part of the truck racks, I climbed the truck racks to free the horses that were still lashed to the top. I pulled out my hunting knife and cut the lead ropes of the horses that had fallen. We were lucky that none of the horses had broken their necks or suffocated. We led all of the horses off the truck by leading them over the rack that was now leaning against the ground. We took them off the truck one

Tales From Working on a Dude Ranch

Richard V. Dalke

by one and handed them over to Jean, who tied them to nearby trees. She'd grabbed extra lead ropes from the back of the pickup for those that needed them. Several of the horses had gashes in their legs and sides. A couple of them were limping badly. The two or three that had fallen were still wheezing and catching their breath, glad to be free of the ropes that had tightened around their necks.

"From now on, I'm just going to load the horses loose inside the truck, not tie them to the side racks. Even if they fall, at least they won't have to labor to breathe or possibly choke to death." Mr. B said sadly as he watched the horses struggle.

I nodded, that wasn't a sight I ever wanted to see again either. After unloading all of the horses, we used the pickup to pull the truck upright again and drove it to a nearby spot where we could reload the horses. They were understandably skittish about getting back on the truck. Mr. B had only cut a few

Richard V. Dalke

of the boards of the truck racks, so they were still solid enough to keep the horses safe once they were reloaded.

We headed back home, that pack trip was over. We needed to take care of the horses the best we could and have a vet come out and check out those with the worst injuries.

One of the horses with the scrapes and cuts was Dan's bay gelding. It was a sad moment when we returned to the ranch and he saw his beloved horse in pain. His pony's injuries healed, but the horse was never quite the same after that.

Mr. B's department store clad friend was never seen on the ranch again.

Richard V. Dalke

Chapter 23

Worth His Weight in Gold

I'd worked on the ranch for 3 summer seasons, and had come back to help out a dozen or more times. It was the middle of the summer and I'd come down to assist the wranglers.

Hope had made an interesting observation when she told me – "how do you always manage to come just when we need you here. One of our wranglers sprained his wrist just a couple of days ago and isn't able to help out as much as he usually does."

Tales From Working on a Dude Ranch

Richard V. Dalke

"Just lucky I guess," I smiled as I answered.

This particular week a very attractive young woman had come to visit for the day. She lived in the Pendleton area and was a friend of the Bakers. She had long blond hair, and was wearing a weathered straw hat, checkered shirt, tight jeans and well-worn riding boots.

I was on my way to bring in the horses who were across the river at the stump farm. I could get to them either by riding a horse across the river or by crossing the bridge that went to the swimming pool and walking along the edge of the river – about ¾ of a mile to where the horses were pasturing. Normally, I would go down to the hay barn and pick out one of the horses that had been left behind and ride it bareback across the river. I would then herd the rest of them back to the feed bunks to get them ready for the next ride.

Tales From Working on a Dude Ranch

Richard V. Dalke

Just as I was stepping out of the tack room with a halter and some horse goodies, the lady from Pendleton walked up and asked if she could go with me. I stammered a yes, as I was still shy, especially around pretty women, but told her that I wasn't planning to ride across the river, as I didn't want to ride any of the horses that were in the corral by the horse barn. I told her I planned to walk across the bridge and alongside the river – a short trek, less than a mile.

"Shouldn't take very long," I told her.

"Not a problem," she said eagerly. "I ride a lot, so I don't have any problem catching a horse and hopping on it bareback." She grabbed a halter and a couple of horse goodies from the tack room and we headed for the bridge.

We started talking and she mentioned that she had met Mr. B in Pendleton and that he had told her that I "was worth my weight in gold." I'd never

Tales From Working on a Dude Ranch

Richard V. Dalke

heard that from Mr. B himself, but was pleased to hear her say that. I wanted to try my hardest to impress her after that statement, but felt even more nervous than before.

I'd never walked alongside the river to get to the stump farm before, so I didn't know what to expect. The brush and trees were as thick as a forest of bramble bushes; what I thought wouldn't take more than 10 or 15 minutes took close to an hour. By the time we reached the horses both of us were scratched, frustrated and dirty. Her hair was full of leaves and stickers, her boots were packed with river mud. She looked a mess by the time we reached the stump farm.

I picked out a horse for her to ride back across the river with and helped her get on; then picked another one for myself. Getting the horses back went without incident, but the riders were all

Tales From Working on a Dude Ranch

wondering what took us so long and were impatiently waiting for us.

Jerry was waiting near the tack room and asked. "You look like a mess. Why didn't you just get a couple of horses from the hay barn to bring in the others." It wouldn't have taken more than 5 or 10 minutes to ride across the river and bring them back."

The lovely lady, covered in leaves and mud looked at me wondering why anyone would think that I was worth my weight in gold, unless they were talking about fool's gold. She slid off her horse, handed me the rope and headed for the ranch house to get cleaned up. I never saw or heard from her again.

Chapter 24

Summer Romances

The ranch was often a magnet for summer romances. A combination of the spectacular beauty of the mountain scenery, the intensity of being together for a short period of time without any of the usual distractions, the adventurous pack trips and trail rides, the warm springs swimming pool at night; all of these made the ranch an enticing place for the wranglers and guests to connect with members of the opposite sex. Each of the wranglers, the girls who worked in the

Tales From Working on a Dude Ranch

kitchen, the single guests – all of us were likely candidates for short term flings.

The difficult part was staying connected with any of these relationships after they returned home. Many of us would try to write, call or even see some of our short term girlfriends and boyfriends, but often we would get distracted by the next group of guests that arrived on Sunday afternoon.

I wrote letters to Becky and Barbara and Kendis and Sue and Laura and Cindy and several other young women I met on the ranch, but bit by bit, each of them went on with their lives and I went on with mine. I continue to have fond memories of each of them and remain grateful for their friendships.

The closest I came to my '15 minutes of fame' happened during one of my summers on the ranch.

Tales From Working on a Dude Ranch

Richard V. Dalke

Hope had come in with the mail one day and made an announcement to the group.

"There's a letter here addressed to Dick the Wrangler, Athena, Oregon. Now who do you suppose that could be for?"

I blushed as I grabbed the letter – it was from one of the girls that I had met at the Bar M, but who didn't know the full address of the ranch.

"Wow, you're practically famous," one of the other wranglers chimed in. "Even the mailman knows who you are, and he delivers mail all over the county. He knew it was for you with just your first name and Athena Oregon written on the front."

I left the room and read the letter in private, smiling that maybe I was just a little bit 'famous'.

Chapter 25

Getting Sunburned

The water that went into the warm-springs swimming pool was hot, so we had to combine it with river water to cool it down to a comfortable temperature. We kept it in the low 90's, a little too warm for some, but just right for me. I loved the warm water, especially swimming in the cool evenings, when steam would rise off the water.

It wasn't very often I got a chance to swim during the daytime, especially when I was working

Richard V. Dalke

as a wrangler. I got my chance years later when my wife and I came down to the ranch as paying guests. Late, one afternoon we went to the pool to enjoy the healing mineral water.

My wife and I swam a few laps across the pool together and then I looked around for an air mattress. My wife got out and lay on a towel at the edge of the pool spreading lotion generously all over herself. I pulled the air mattress into the pool and climbed on top of it, stretching out and relaxing, enjoying the 90 degree weather. I'll just be here a few minutes, I thought, I won't need any suntan lotion.

I soon fell asleep and didn't wake up for almost an hour. I felt a little uncomfortable then, but didn't know until later just how bad I'd gotten sunburned. My skin was beet red, from head to toe.

When I woke up the next morning, I could barely move, but my wife was very eager to go

Tales From Working on a Dude Ranch

Richard V. Dalke

horseback riding that day. She wanted to make sure we never missed a ride the entire week and didn't want to ride with a large group. We were allowed to go by ourselves since I had been a wrangler for 3 seasons, knew the trails well and knew what to expect from the horses.

After getting our horses ready, I climbed very gently into the saddle, sitting very still so as not to move any of my sunburned parts any farther than I needed to.

Later that day, after returning from the ride, I went down to the hay barn to see what the wranglers were doing. They wanted me to help unload the hay, along with catching them up on what I'd been up to since my last visit.

I was reluctant to let them know how foolish I'd been laying in the sun that long. I clambered up the front of the truck to the top of the hay bales. Grabbing a pair of hay hooks, I started unloading

Tales From Working on a Dude Ranch

Richard V. Dalke

the 80 lb. bales of hay. They didn't have any extra hay aprons that I could wear which might have given me a little protection from the protruding alfalfa stems. So each time I lifted one of the bales of hay, I could feel the excruciating pain through my denim jeans, rubbing against my sunburned legs.

"You're awfully quiet." noted Jerry. "You're usually quite talkative when you're helping us unload the hay."

"I got a bit sunburned yesterday when I was swimming in the pool," I offered through clenched teeth, trying to sound somewhat normal.

"Yeah, that probably wouldn't feel very good. You did put sun tan lotion on though, right?"

"Right." I grimaced. I could tell they weren't about to let me off the hook by finishing the job themselves. I knew the unspoken rule. When it's time to work, you complete the job, without

Richard V. Dalke

complaining or whining. We finished unloading the hay and I lumbered all the way down the driveway and went in for lunch.

It took the rest of the week before my sunburn healed enough to peel and stop hurting. I have never slept on that or any other air mattress in a pool since.

Chapter 26

Viewing From a Higher Level

Most of the trail rides were appropriate for any of our guests. However we had a few trails we used only for the more experienced riders. One of these more difficult rides was to Bear Creek Falls. We headed up river and went through the first gate at Bear Creek, but instead of heading up the hill to the north slope, we went through a second gate and followed the creek a couple of miles. We crossed the creek numerous times before we got to the falls. The falls were

Tales From Working on a Dude Ranch

Richard V. Dalke

spectacular, especially early in the spring, as Bear Creek was full from the fresh snow melt. The water spilled over the edge of the rocks, splashed down into a pool, ran under a log at the edge and continued on down to the Umatilla River. We would ride within a hundred yards or so of the falls, and then tie our horses to the birch and willow trees nearby. The first time I saw the falls, I was entranced.

On the second or third time I visited the falls, I decided to try something new. I sat on a rock next to the quick-splashing waterfall and stared into the pool. I then closed my eyes and meditated. I didn't really know how to meditate, but it felt like the right thing to do. I let my mind quiet itself and just watched the thoughts flow through my awareness, without trying to control them or stop them. It was magical. Soon after that, I also started

Richard V. Dalke

writing poetry, inspired by the feelings I felt next to the running water.

There were times when I felt that same meditative stillness when on the trail with the guests. A few months after I'd started meditating and writing poetry, I was going on a trail ride on a beautiful summer afternoon. I was riding in the middle of the pack, so I could relax a bit from the responsibilities of being in the lead or at the end. We were riding on the north slope, the weather was perfect. The temperature was in the 80's, there was a slight breeze, a cerulean blue sky, a few small cumulus clouds overhead.

A young couple in their 30's had come for the day with a female friend who was in her late 20's. The couple were friends of Mr. B's who lived in Portland. Wendy, the couple's friend, had long blond hair and a cute smile. I was smitten.

Tales From Working on a Dude Ranch

Richard V. Dalke

When we got to the top of the hill, coming across the flat part of the trail, I felt like I was in some kind of trance. My energy level quickened, my senses were heightened. I could hear more clearly, my sight was enhanced, my feelings were intensified. I was experiencing what I learned later Abraham Maslow calls a 'peak experience.' I felt totally alert, not from an adrenaline rush like I got from racing my horse on the mountainside, but in a meditative, completely alive kind of way. My mind was quiet from observing the beauty around me. All I could think was "WOW" to everything I noticed around me. I was not stoned on alcohol or drugs, I was just totally tuned in to what I call my "Higher Self." It was awesome.

After the ride was over, I asked Wendy if she had felt anything special about that trip.

"I did," she answered, but looked a little shy about sharing that with me. A month or so later,

Tales From Working on a Dude Ranch

Richard V. Dalke

after the summer season was over at the ranch, I drove to Portland to stay for a short time with the young couple and got to meet Wendy again. I found out she had a boyfriend, one she had known for years.

I was still grateful, as my attraction to her had helped me feel a very special connection – with nature, with beauty, with myself. To this day, I remember this experience as a 'touchstone' to help me feel connected to my inner spirit and to experience the world from a higher vantage point.

Since then, I've written two volumes of poetry and a few other nonfiction books reflecting the life philosophies I've developed over the years. I still meditate on a regular basis and feel inspired whenever I remember the Bar M. The wallpaper on my computer is the picture I took of the Umatilla River that appears in the front of this book, which I see and appreciate every day.

Tales From Working on a Dude Ranch

Richard V. Dalke

I never went back to the riding stable where I'd applied for a job so many years before and was turned down. That experience inspired my journey which led me to the Bar M. As a result, I feel I was able to fulfill the promise I'd made to myself so many years earlier.

I learned a lot on the Bar M, not only about horses and cattle, but more importantly, about making short term and life-long friends, how to work responsibly, how to grow from a boy into a man and how to get in touch with my inner spirit. I shall be forever grateful for the adventures and friendships I experienced there which helped me achieve this personal and spiritual growth.

Tales From Working on a Dude Ranch

Richard V. Dalke

This book is available through amazon.com
and other book retailers.

Richard V. Dalke

About The Author

Richard Dalke has his Master's degree in Counseling Psychology and has been a counselor for over 29 years. Prior to that time, he worked at many kinds of jobs, including dance instructor, wrangler, biofeedback therapist, salesman, minister, auctioneer, taxi driver, bus driver, long haul truck driver, dairy farmer, and others. He currently works as a care advocate, voice over artist and author. You can learn more about him by visiting his website at deerhawkenterprises.com.

His interests include drumming, riding his Honda Goldwing motorcycle, helping out on his brother's cattle ranch and spending quality time with his family.

He currently lives with his wife in Spokane, WA.